Ghosts and and Things With O's

by Leonard Kessler

SCHOLASTIC BOOK SERVICES
NEW YORK · TORONTO · LONDON · AUCKLAND · SYDNEY · TOKYO

ISBN: 0-590-00274-0

12 11 10 9 8   0 1/8

This is not an **A** book
This is not a **B** book
This is not a **C** book
This is not a **D** book
This is not an **E** book
This is not an **F** book
This is not a **G** book
This is not an **H** book
This is not an **I** book
This is not a **J** book
This is not a **K** book
This is not an **L** book
This is not an **M** book
This is not an **N** book

It's a book about O's.

I don't see any O's,
do you?

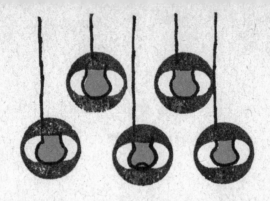

Anybody see any O's around here?

Do you see any O's
down by the sea?

When the circus comes to town,
can you find any O's?

Up in the air,
Down on the ground,
Can you find
any O's around?

What do you say to a sad chair?

Chair up!

Do you see any O's
going up and down a hill?

Oh I don't care about O's.
Who needs O's?

I'll tell you who needs O's.
You do!

Ghosts need O's
to go BOO.

Trains need O's to go
CHOO CHOO CHOO.

Sign painters need O's, too.

ONE WAY

STOP

SCHOOL

PEOPLE
WORKING

There are times when
nothing but O's will do!

You need O's
to write
frog
dog
hog
log.

**You need more O's
to write
crook
took
book.**

You need one O for Hippo,
Two O's for Zoo,
One O for Owl,
And two for Kangaroo.

And here's something else.
Do you want to know?

O   O   O

You need O's to play Tic Tac Toe!

**How many
O words
do you know?**

O words

Boo to
you,
too!

Boo!

more O words

**Now you can choose a letter
and make your own book.**